The Next Generation Science Standards (NGSS) are reproduced with permission from the Department of Education.

Written by Jake Hunter, Toben Hunter, and Aysha Imtiaz.

Illustrations by Bella Hunter, watercolors by Lilly Hunter.

Choose a Purpose for a Material: Toby Tee's Super Duper Slip 'N Slide Shoes

Student Edition

ISBN 978-1-952346-43-9

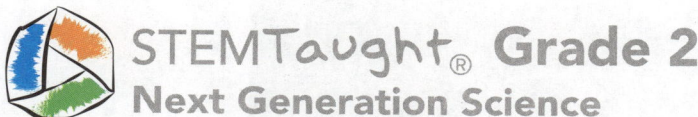 **STEMTaught**® **Grade 2**
Next Generation Science

2-PS1-2 Matter and Its Interactions: Analyze data obtained from testing different materials to determine which materials have the properties that are best suited for an intended purpose.

The Rice Lifting Challenge

Toby loves to do magic tricks.

"Ladies and Gentlemen," Toby said. "For my next trick, I will lift a container full of rice with my pencil! First I will stick this ordinary pencil down into the rice and then I will simply lift up. Watch for it... Watch for it... And, tadaa! I did it!" Toby lifted his container of rice high into the air.

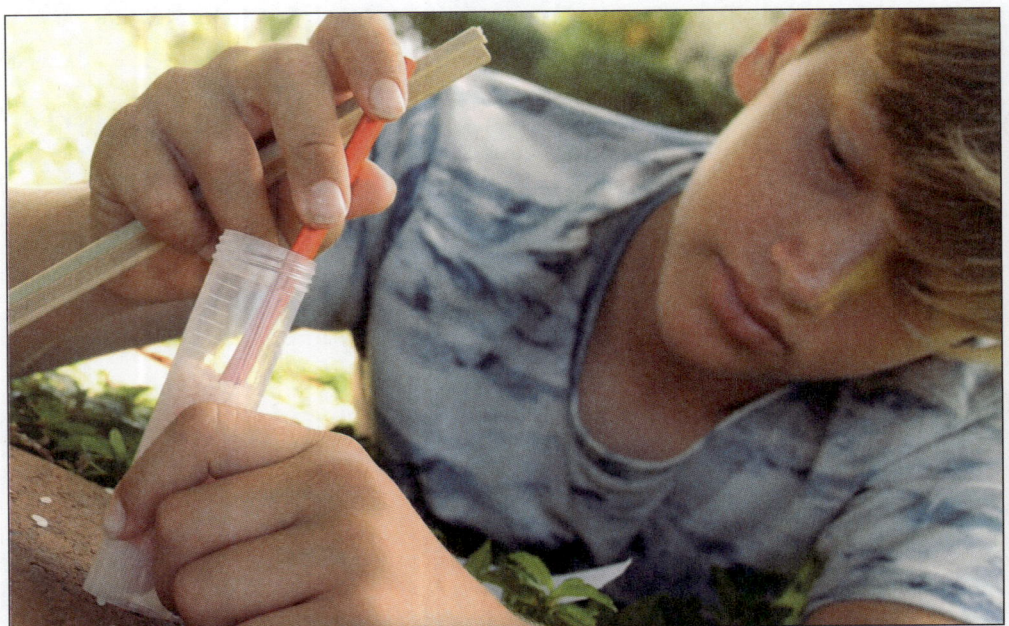
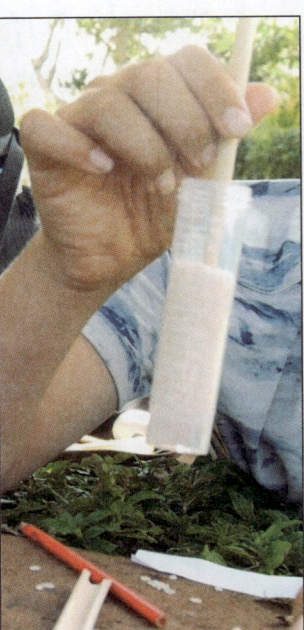

This is Toby experimenting to see if he can lift a test tube full of rice with an ordinary pencil.

Amazing! How did he do it! Do you think it is magic? Or, could you do it too? Try it for yourself! Experiment!

What you need:

- Scissors to cut your funnel

- One Tedros test tube (or a tall container)

- Rice or sand (enough to fill most of your container)

- Various materials (a pencil, chopstick, leaf, twig, or a strip of paper)

What you will do:

1. Cut out and tape your funnel.

2. Put rice or sand into your container using your paper funnel.

3. Insert a pencil into the rice.

4. Try lifting up the pencil.

MY FUNNEL

Instructions:
1. Cut
2. Overlap
3. Tape or glue

Overlap area

Can the pencil lift up the container of rice? Try tapping the container on the ground to help the rice settle and try lifting again.

3

Experiment some more

Okay, was that too easy? Well, then, experiment some more. What other types of objects or materials can you use to lift the container of rice?

Make careful observations as you try more materials!

Can you lift it with a chopstick?

A thick stick?

A thin stick?

A plant stem?

A strip of paper?

A plastic pen?

A piece of metal (butter knife)?

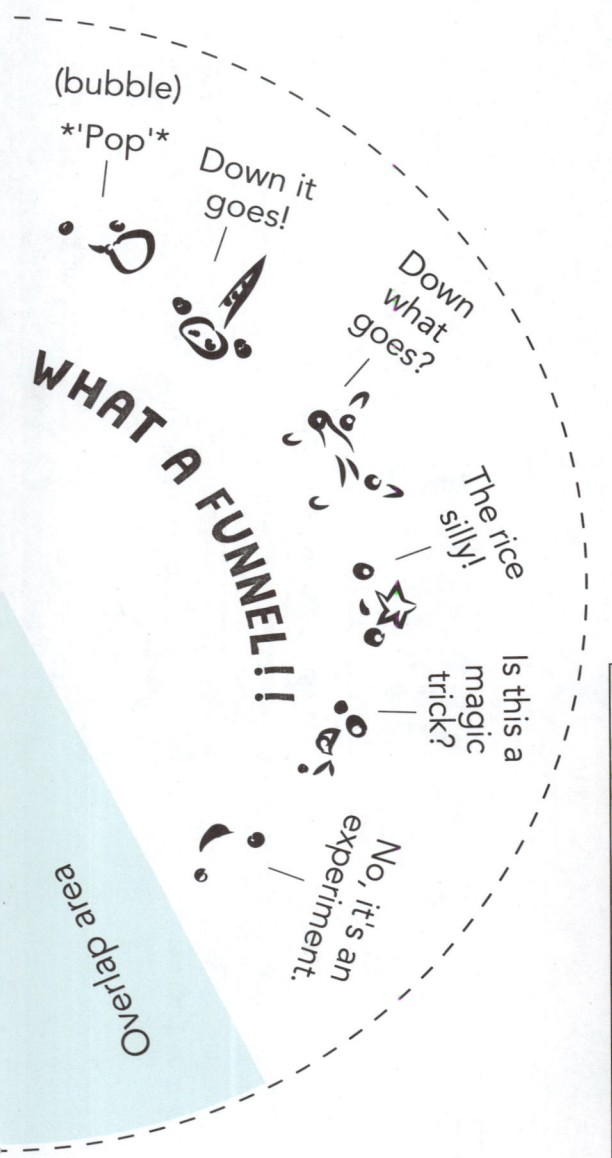

(bubble)

'Pop'

Down it goes!

Down what goes?

The rice silly!

Is this a magic trick?

No, it's an experiment.

WHAT A FUNNEL!!

Overlap area

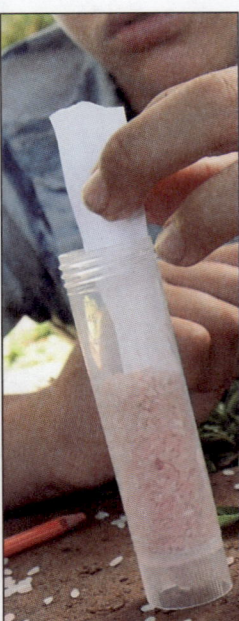

chopstick   **twig**   **paper**

Your observations

What materials work best to lift the container of rice? Draw your results.

How does the pencil lift the container full of rice?

_____

_____

_____

_____

How does the pencil lift the container full of rice?

Think, Pair, Share!

Friction takes the slip out of your slide!

Friction happens when objects rub against each other. Objects that are smooth slide against each other easily and have very little friction. The steel blades of an ice skate slide easily across the ice and have very little friction.

The steel blades of ice skates slip across the ice easily.

Less Friction

Objects that grip surfaces well or seem rough create friction. The rubber soles of hiking boots grip the ground with friction so the hiker does not slip.

The rubber soles of hiking boots grip the ground well.

More Friction

Slip? Or Grip?

Identify which objects have more or less friction.

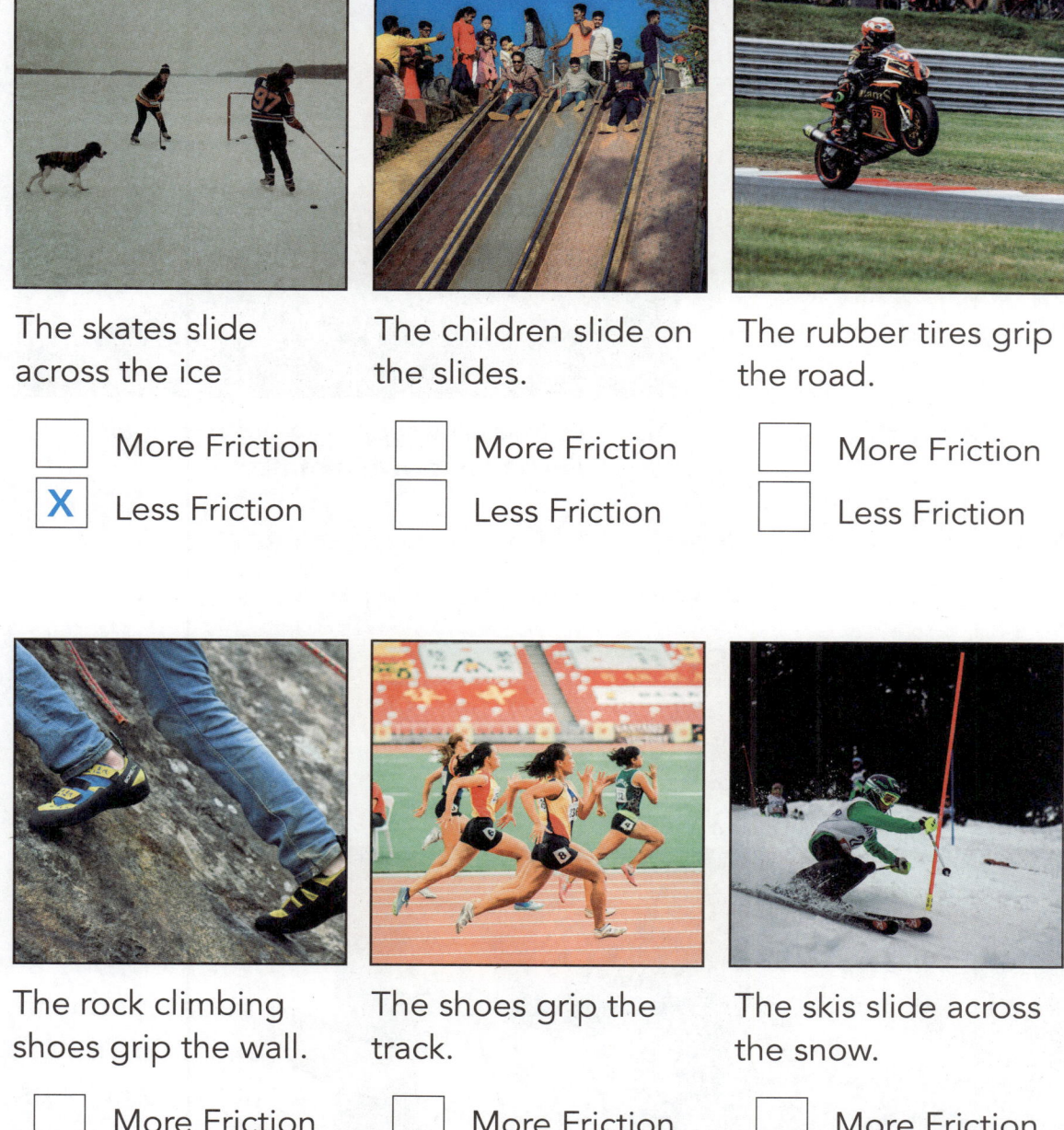

The skates slide across the ice

- [ ] More Friction
- [X] Less Friction

The children slide on the slides.

- [ ] More Friction
- [ ] Less Friction

The rubber tires grip the road.

- [ ] More Friction
- [ ] Less Friction

The rock climbing shoes grip the wall.

- [ ] More Friction
- [ ] Less Friction

The shoes grip the track.

- [ ] More Friction
- [ ] Less Friction

The skis slide across the snow.

- [ ] More Friction
- [ ] Less Friction

You will experiment with friction

In this unit, you will test different materials by sliding them down a ramp. After testing your materials you will know which materials slide easily and have the least amount of friction.

You can test how slippery your materials are by sliding them down a ramp.

You will read a story about a Hawaiian green sea turtle named Toby Tee. As you follow along with the story, you will do your own experimenting.

HONU
Hawaiian for sea turtle

Sea turtles all over the world are threatened with extinction due to human activities. We must protect these endangered animals.

Get ready to measure angles

You will get to measure angles with a protractor as you experiment. When you measure an angle, it will tell you how steeply your ramp is tipped. A protractor can help you measure this angle. We measure angles with a protractor in degrees.

Practice reading the protractor. Each line on the protractor is one degree.

What angle is this?

What angle is this?

What angle is this?

A protractor is a tool that we use to measure angles.

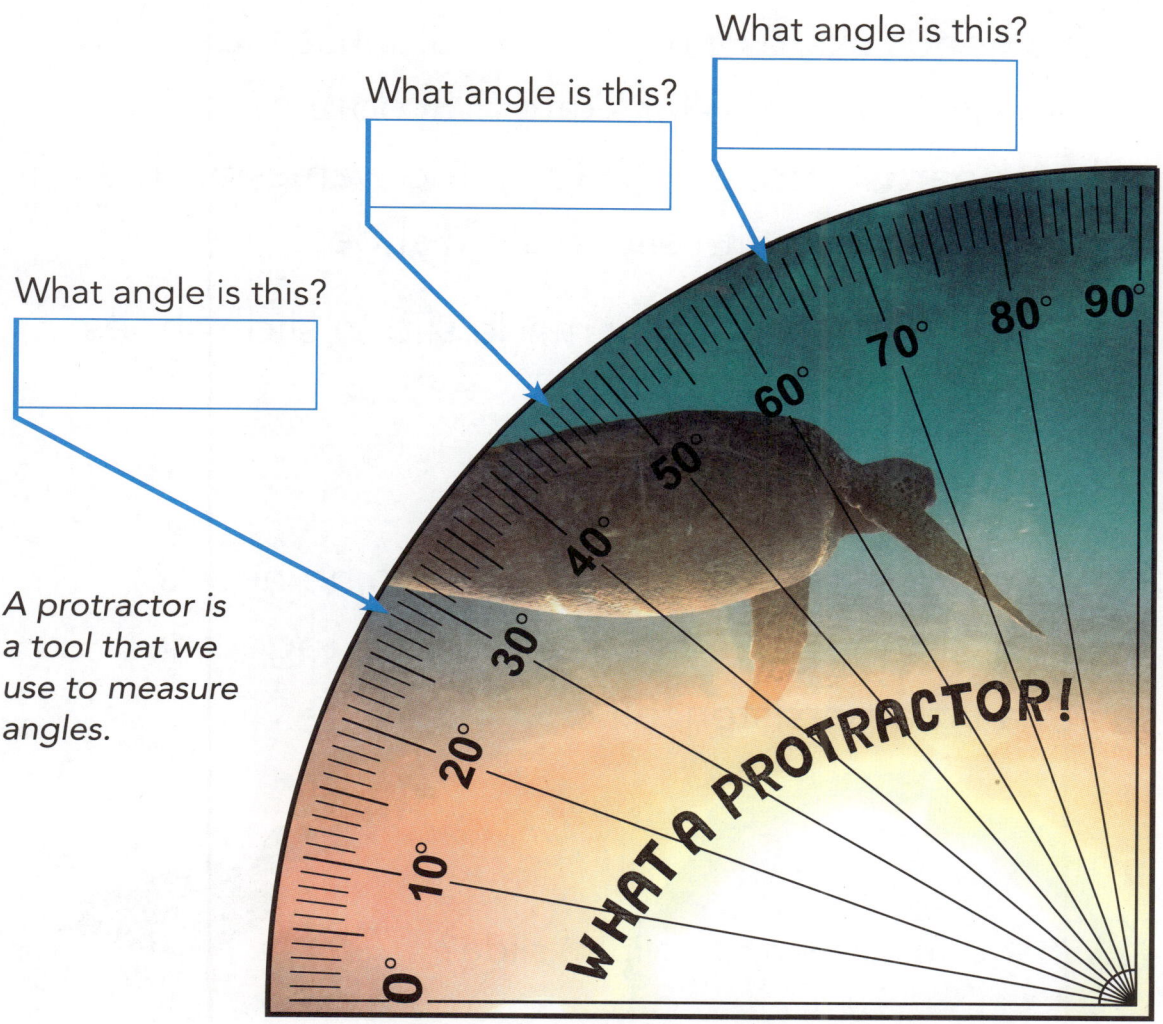

Cut out the protractor from the back cover of your book.

Toby Tee's Super-Duper Slip 'N Slide Shoes

By Jake Hunter, Toben Hunter and Aysha Imtiaz

Illustrated by Toby, Bella, Lilly and Beth Hunter

Introduction:

Who needs skates when you could just slide all around town? Roller skates? Scooters? Skateboards? No, pooh! Toby Tee wants to slide all around town with slip 'n slide shoes!

But wait! Toby has never made slip 'n slide shoes before.

Have you?

Before Toby can make his invention he needs your assistance! We can figure it out together, with a little persistence!

What does it mean to slip n' slide?

Think, Pair, Share!

Part 1:

Good ideas can come from anywhere!

Let me start by telling you how Toby Tee got his most magnificent idea ever!

Everything Toby Tee ever did was a grand adventure. Toby Tee was an expert at having fun wherever he went.

But ... it was shopping day and even though Toby wanted to play with his new, home-made gummy bear blaster, it was time to go to the store with his mother.

Think, Pair, Share!

Where did you get your last cool idea?

"Can I look at the list?" Toby asked excitedly. "We're going to the market to get taro, mangoes, rice and cheese? ..."

"... But wait, Mom! There are no treats on this list!" Toby smiled his sweetest smile. For a moment, he truly looked like a little angel. "May I add cheese puffs to the list, please?"

"Only healthy foods today," said Mom.

'This is going to be the worst shopping trip ever,' Toby thought to himself.

They walked down the aisles and Toby's mom put food into the cart.

With a little toss, in went the taro, the mangoes and then the cheese.

"Please! No icky cold cheese," Toby begged. "I don't like cheese... Well, I only like it when it's melted on a pizza like hot, bubbly, molten lava. And, I like cheese puffs too, of course!" said Toby.

Toby was riding on the shopping cart while he talked and his mother pushed.

"Mom, can you push a little faster, please? I want to drag my feet to slip and slide along the floor like a ...."

And *that* was the moment when Toby had the most awesomest idea ever!

"Ladies and gentlemen," Toby proudly announced. "Now, I will slip and slide across the grocery store floor!"

What makes something slippery or not?

Think, Pair, Share!

16

He jumped down from the cart to try the best slide of his life!

"This is going to be the most magnificent slide of the year!" he announced. "Or, of the century... Or of forever!"

He started to run down the isle, then, 'grrr-rrr-raaaate' his flippers did not slide as well as he had expected. Instead of sliding, he fell on the ground with a great thud.

"Well, I know," he said as he got back up, "It wasn't that great. It could be better! But, Mom! Now, I can't wait to go home to find slippery materials to make slip 'n slide shoes!"

Why do you think Toby fell down?

Think, Pair, Share!

19

Part 2:

Friction, you took the slip right out of my slide!

The next day Toby was telling his cousin about what happened. "I need something to reduce friction so I can slide!" Toby said.

"What is friction?" his cousin asked.

"Let me teach you about friction," Toby said. "Friction is when two objects rub against each other and slow each other down. Let me show you. I'll be object A and the ground is object B. Push me and see how this grumpy-fuss friction is stopping me from slipping and sliding all around."

Toby felt his shell rubbing across the ground.

"Oh yes, friction! I feel you!" he said. "I am going to get rid of all friction!" Toby said. "We need to find something slippery so the new slip n' slide shoes will work."

Where have you seen or felt friction happen?

Think, Pair, Share!

20

Part 3:

How to measure friction

"How slippery is something? That is the question we need to answer. To find the answer we can use another amazing invention of mine! It's my very own, handy dandy slip-o-meter!"

Toby raced to his toy bin and found Roxy ramp and Blocky, his two favorite toys. For everyone out there reading this right now, you can make your very own slip-o-meter too. You will need:

- Blocky (a wooden block or something flat to slide)

- Roxy ramp (a ramp or something flat that you can tilt)

- A protractor to measure the angle of slip.

You can find a protractor on the back cover of your book.

How can you tell how much friction something has?

Think, Pair, Share!

22

By experimenting with different materials to observe how slippery or not slippery they are, you can help design the best slip 'n slide shoes ever!

Now that you have your stuff, here's what you will do:

1. Put the material to be tested onto the bottom of Blocky.

2. Partner 1 places Blocky on Roxy ramp and slowly lifts one end of the ramp. Watch for the moment that Blocky starts to slip. When you see it start to slip, hold the ramp in place.

3. Partner 2 uses the protractor to measure the angle that Blocky starts to slip.

Part 4:

The great slip-o-meter experiment:

Testing wood

Toby Tee was ready to test his first material. He would test Blocky. Blocky was made of wood.

"How slippery or not slippery is a piece of wood? That is the question I need to answer with my very own slip-o-meter!" Toby said as he placed Blocky on Roxy ramp. He slowly began to lift one end of the ramp.

Oh, the suspense! What will the angle of slip turn out to be?!

And then, 'phhhsssss-sssshhhh'—slip. When he saw Blocky begin to slip, he held the ramp frozen in place as he measured the ramp's angle with his handy dandy protractor.

Tip: The ramp end should be touching the corner of the protractor when taking a measurement.

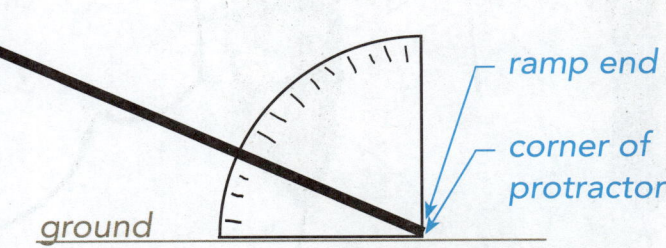

WOOD

Glue Sample Here!

Write angle of slip here:

What does a high angle of slip measurement mean for slipperiness?

Think, Pair, Share!

Part 5:

The great slip-o-meter experiment:

Testing cardboard

Now Toby wanted to try another material. He went to his kitchen to find the perfect thing, and there it was sitting on the counter—a cereal box!

"How slippery or not slippery is cardboard from a cereal box? That is the question I need to answer," Toby said.

He cut a piece of cardboard and taped it to the bottom of Blocky. He set Blocky down and slowly began to lift one end of the ramp.

Wait for it... Wait for it… And then, 'phhhsssss-sssshhhh'—slip.

Toby was the master at measuring! He wrote down the angle in his journal.

Is your cereal box more slippery or less slippery than the wood?

Think, Pair, Share!

Part 6:

The great slip-o-meter experiment:

Testing tin foil

The cardboard was fun but now Toby wanted to try something else. Toby searched through his kitchen until he found a piece of shiny tin foil. The tin foil felt smooth, just like a playground slide.

"How slippery is tin foil? That is the question!" Toby said as he cut a piece of tin foil and wrapped it around Blocky.

Toby used his best pilot voice, "Ladies and gentlemen, this is Captain Tee speaking. We are ready for takeoff."

'Da da da da da da da,' (Drum roll)

Toby lifted the ramp higher and higher, and then 'sssssssss'—slip. 'Wheeeeee-e!' The slide!

How long do you think tin foil would last on the bottom of your shoes? Why?

Think, Pair, Share!

Part 7:

The great slip-o-meter experiment:

Testing plastic

Toby was searching for the next material to test. Before long he found it—plastic! The plastic felt smooth to touch, but also seemed very tough. Toby was sure that plastic was his anti-friction material. This was going to be amazing!

"How slippery or not slippery is plastic? That is the question. To find the answer, I will use my very own slip-o-meter!"

Toby cut a piece of plastic and wrapped it around Blocky. He carefully lifted one end of Roxy ramp. Before long he saw Blocky slip!

Yesssss! That measurement seemed pretty good. Finally, he felt like he was making progress!

What types of plastic materials could you test?

Think, Pair, Share!

PLASTIC

Glue Sample Here!

Write angle of slip here:

Part 8:

The best material that I know

'I need these shoes to be so slippery and fast,' Toby thought. Inventors know that to find the best option, we must try, and try again.

Toby searched all around for the best material to test. Guess what material he found!

Choose a material that you want to test.

What material did you find?

Draw your material here.

Why do you think your material will work well?

_____

_____

Glue
Sample
Here!

Write angle
of slip here:

Part 9:

And the winner is ...

Now, after your amazing experimenting, we will choose the best material tested so far! Remember all those slip-o-meter measurements you collected? That is called data. Data is only helpful when you organize it, otherwise it's just a bunch of numbers.

Organize your data below and then plot each number on the graph.

 List your angle of slip measurements from smallest to largest.

	Material Tested	Angle of Slip	
1.			small #
2.			
3.			
4.			
5.			large #

Why is it a good idea to sort your measurements and list them in order?

Think, Pair, Share!

 Make a graph to show the slipperiness of your materials. Color in the white area up to the angle of slip you measured for each material.

How Slippery My Materials Are

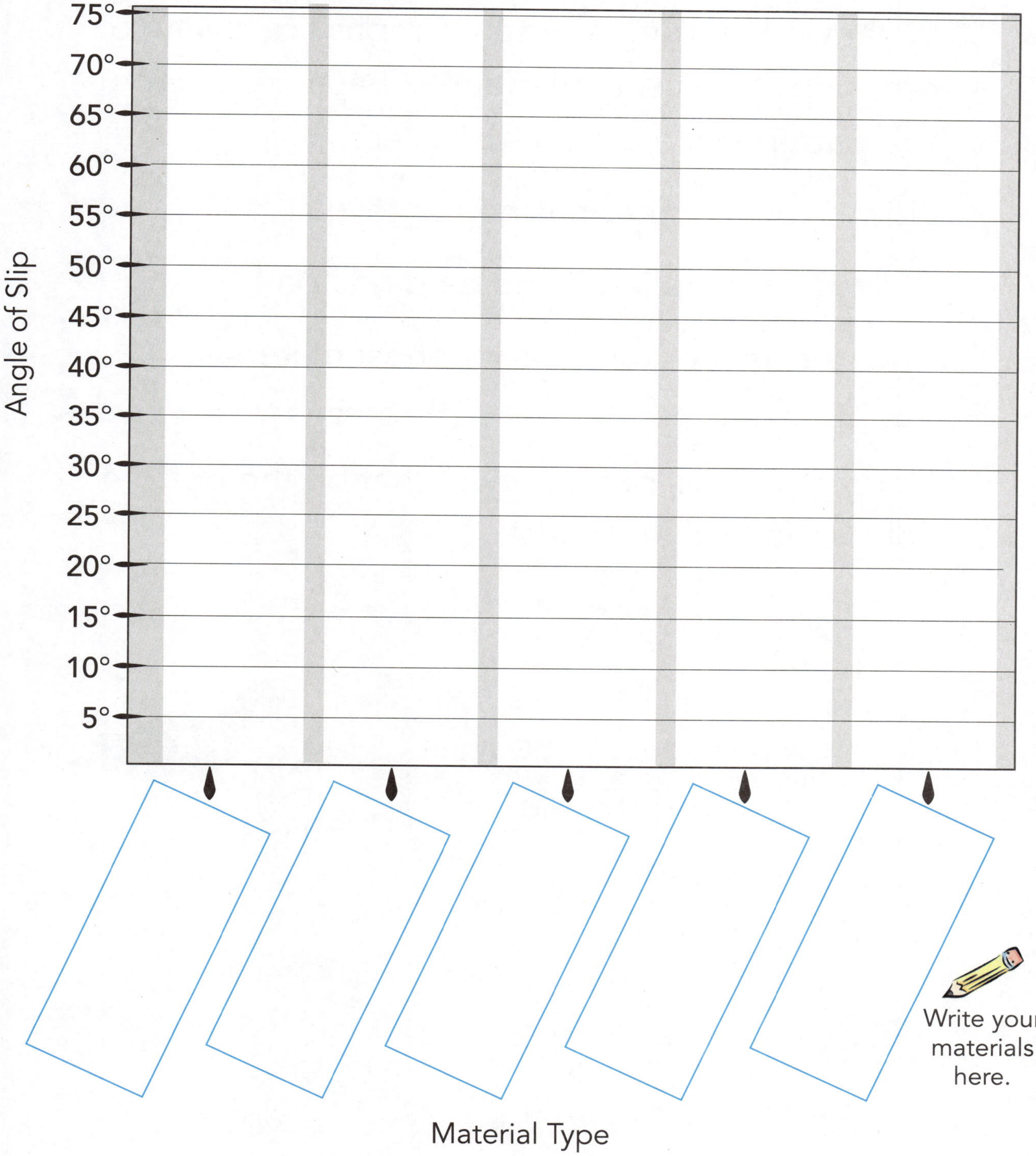

Angle of Slip

75°
70°
65°
60°
55°
50°
45°
40°
35°
30°
25°
20°
15°
10°
5°

Write your
materials
here.

Material Type

Great work making a graph! Graphs are a way to draw a picture using numbers! Graphs can help us see patterns in the data we collect.

Now is the moment for the big reveal!

Ready? Drum roll—'Da da da da da da!'

And, the winner for the slipperiest material is _____! (write the winning material here.)

Hooray! We will put plenty of that on the bottom of Toby's slip 'n slide shoes!

How did you decide what material to use?

Think, Pair, Share!

Part 10:

Aaaand....Wheeeee! They work!

Thank you so much for your help experimenting with different materials. Guess what? It's grocery shopping day again. It's time to test out the new slip 'n slide shoes.

Toby ran into the grocery store with his new shoes and announced, "Look here, everyone! This is going to be epic! Legendary! The most magnificent slide of the year!"

"Aaaand....Wheeeee!"

"They work!"

"Mom, I don't mind going to the grocery store anymore. Can we go shopping every day?" Toby asked. "THIS IS SO FUN!"

What other things would you consider when choosing the best material?

Think, Pair, Share!

Featured Author

Toby

Having fun is Toby's best talent! He wanted to make a touch/feel and experiment book for you. He helped write the book and draw the pictures in it. Toby wants to be an engineer when he grows up. He likes exploring in the jungles of Hawaii with his dog where he finds amazing animals like this chameleon.

Bella

Lilly

Meet the artists

Bella illustrates and Lilly brings the illustrations to life with watercolor paints. Bella wants to study birds when she grows up. She wants to help endangered species. Lilly loves training animals and has trained a seeing eye dog.

Endangered monk seal pups nap on the beach on the island of Oahu.

Hawaiian ecosystems are delicate

This book features animals that live on the Hawaiian Islands. Some of the animals you will see are native to the islands and others were introduced here by humans. Many of the native animals in Hawaii are endangered, meaning that very few of their species are left alive. These animals have become endangered because of human activities such as habitat loss due to building houses, the introduction of non-native species, and hunting. Endangered animals must be protected if they are to survive. Do you love animals? Maybe you could become a scientist that studies and protects these beautiful animals.

Can you find me in the story?

The illustrations in this book feature animals found in the Hawaiian Islands. The animals on these two pages are native to the islands while the animals on the next two pages were brought to the islands by humans.

Check off the animals that you find in the illustrations of the story!

ILIO KAI ☐
Hawaiian Monk Seal

MOLI ☐
Laysan Albatross

Hawaiians call the monk seal "ilio holo i ka uaua," which means "dog that runs in rough water". The Hawaiian monk seal is one of the most endangered marine mammals in the world. They are threatened with extinction due to human activities. There are only 1,500 Hawaiian monk seals left in existence today.

With a 6 foot wingspan, the Laysan Albatross are among the largest seabirds. Hawaiians call these birds "moli." Moli are excellent at soaring and can remain flying both day and night. They commonly fly from Hawaii to Alaskan waters (1000 miles) to find squid to bring back to their nesting chicks in Hawaii.

NENE ☐
Hawaiian Goose

The Nene gets its name from its soft call. In 1952 its population had been reduced to 30 birds. The population today stands at 1,500 birds, making it the world's most endangered goose.

ALEA'ULA ☐
Hawaiian Moorhen

The Alea'ula is a very secretive waterfowl that is considered sacred in Hawaiian legends. In the 1960s only 57 remained, making them a critically endangered species.

I'IWI ☐
Hawaiian Honeycreeper

Twenty species of Honeycreepers have recently become extinct and the remaining types are endangered.

IWA ☐
Black Frigate Bird

The Iwa gets its name from the Hawaiian word for "thief". It commonly forces other birds to drop their catch.

LOLE MANAKUKE ☐
Indian Mongoose

The mongoose was introduced to the Hawaiian islands in 1833. As a non-native species, mongoose are harmful to native bird populations.

PUA'A ☐
Wild Boar

Ancient Hawaiians brought pigs to the islands more than 800 years ago. "Pua'a" means pig.

CHAMELEON ☐
Jackson Chameleon

Chameleons were released in Oahu by a pet shop in 1972. Now they live all over the Hawaiian Islands.

GECKO ☐
Gold Dust Gecko

The gold dust gecko was introduced from Madagascar to the islands of Hawaii.

CARDINAL ☐
Red Crested Cardinal

The red crested cardinal was introduced to the islands in the 1930s.

BULBUL ☐
Red Whiskered Bulbul

The Indian red whiskered bulbul was illegally introduced to the Hawaiian islands in the 1960s. They compete with native birds.

KAUAI CHICKEN ☐
Red Jungle Fowl

Ancient Hawaiians introduced the red jungle fowl to the islands over 800 years ago.

ANOLE ☐
Brown Anole

The brown anole is native to the Caribbean and was accidentally introduced to Hawaii in the 1980s.

I'm hungry after all that experimenting

Experimenting is hard work! It makes me hungry! How about you? Since you have been observing Hawaiian wildlife in the paintings, I thought I would share a recipe for a famous Hawaiian snack. Try cooking this delicious snack at home with your parents!

PONO'S SPAM MUSUBI

What you need:

- Spam

- Cooked rice (sticky Jasmine or Calrose rice)

- Nori (seaweed paper)

- Teriyaki sauce (soy sauce mixed with sugar)

What you will do:

1. Cut Spam into slices.

2. Cook Spam and drizzle teriyaki sauce on it.

3. Press and shape a patty of rice to be the same size as a piece of spam.

4. Layer the Spam and rice like a sandwich and wrap in nori seaweed. Aloha musubi!

Try this authentic Hawaiian treat—Spam musubi.

Can you explain it?

Now that you have learned about friction, let's revisit the rice trick you did at the beginning of the unit. How did the pencil lift the container of rice? The rice grains create enough friction against the pencil to keep it from slipping out of the container.

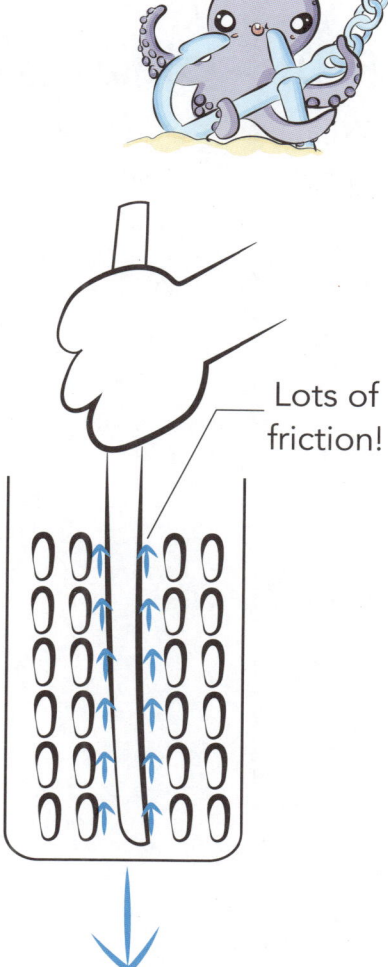

Lots of friction!

The weight of the rice and container.

Think, Pair, Share!

How did the pencil lift the container full of rice?

Which material was best for lifting the rice?

_____

Why is the material you chose good for lifting rice grains?

_____

_____

_____

_____

Fun-Dixie Journal Entry

What was your favorite part of learning in this chapter? Draw and write about your experiences.

**Royal
STEMTaught Post**

When you read a great chapter in the STEMTaught Journal and do the fun activities inside, sometimes you just want to write about it!